Discovering
Cultures

# South Africa

Patricia J. Murphy

**BENCHMARK BOOKS**

MARSHALL CAVENDISH
NEW YORK

*For my niece, Olivia, with love—P.J.M.*

Benchmark Books
Marshall Cavendish
99 White Plains Road
Tarrytown, New York 10591-9001
www.marshallcavendish.com

All Internet sites were available and accurate when sent to press.

Library of Congress Cataloging-in-Publication Data

Murphy, Patricia J., 1963–
South Africa / by Patricia J. Murphy.
p. cm. — (Discovering cultures)
Summary: An introduction to the history, geography, language, schools, and social life and customs of South Africa.
Includes bibliographical references and index.
ISBN 0-7614-1719-2
1. South Africa—Juvenile literature. [1. South Africa.] I. Title.
II. Series.
DT1719.M87 2003
968—dc21                          2003008129

Photo Research by Candlepants Incorporated
Cover Photo: Bob Krist / *Corbis*

The photographs in this book are used by permission and through the courtesy of; *Index Stock*: Zefa Visual Media, 1; W. Bibikow, 4. *Corbis*: Charles O' Rear, 6 (top), 14, 36, 43 (top left); Anthony Bannister/Gallo Images, 7, 17; Nigel J. Dennis/Gallo Images, 8; Earl & Nazima Kowall, 11, 43 (lower left); Roger De La Harpe/Gallo Images, 12, 16, 18, 33, 34; David Turnley, 13, 45 (left); Caroline Penn, 26; Owen Franklin, 27 (top); Reuters NewMedia Inc., 28, 31, 38, 45 (right); AFP, 30, 32, 37 (right), 43 (lower right) Durand Patrick/Sygma, 44; *Jason Laure*: 6, (lower), 10, 20, 24. *The Image Works*: Marcel & Eva Malherbe, 9, 42 (right); Louis Gubb, 19, 21, 22, 27 (lower), 37 (left), back cover. *Lucid Images/ Mark Downey*: 15; *Friedrich Stark/Peter Arnold*: 23.

Cover: *The Afrikaans Language Monument in Paarl, South Africa*; Title page: *A young woman wearing traditional beads*

Map and illustrations by Ian Warpole
Book design by Virginia Pope

Printed in China
1  3  5  6  4  2

# Turn the Pages...

# Where in the World
# Is South Africa?

The Republic of South Africa is at the southern tip of Africa. If you traveled any further south, you would fall right into the ocean! Water touches much of South Africa. The Atlantic Ocean is to the west. The Indian Ocean is to the south and east.

South Africa is separated from the rest of Africa by rivers. The Limpopo, Orange, and Vaal Rivers run along the edges of the country. South Africa's neighbors include Botswana, Zimbabwe, Namibia, Mozambique, the Kingdom of Swaziland, and the State of Lesotho. Lesotho is completely surrounded by South Africa. The Kalahari Desert brushes the northern part of South Africa. Along the coast, there are miles of sandy beaches.

*An ocean view from the South African coast*

4

# Map of South Africa

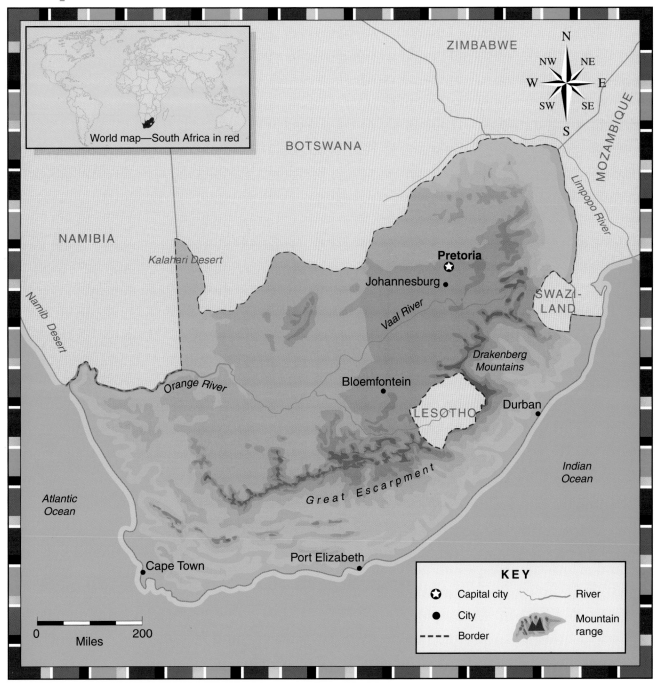

World map—South Africa in red

ZIMBABWE

BOTSWANA

NAMIBIA

MOZAMBIQUE

Limpopo River

*Kalahari Desert*

**Pretoria**

Johannesburg

Vaal River

SWAZI-LAND

Namib Desert

*Drakenberg Mountains*

*Orange River*

Bloemfontein

Durban

LESOTHO

Indian Ocean

Atlantic Ocean

*G r e a t   E s c a r p m e n t*

Cape Town

Port Elizabeth

**KEY**

⬡ Capital city

● City

--- Border

River

Mountain range

0    Miles    200

N
NW    NE
W         E
SW    SE
S

*Red sand dunes in the desert*

*Downtown Cape Town*

South Africa has three capital cities: Cape Town, Pretoria, and Bloemfontein. Each of these cities has a different job. Cape Town is where laws are made. Pretoria is where business is done. Bloemfontein is where judges hold court. Johannesburg is South Africa's largest city.

The country of South Africa measures 471,445 square miles (1,221,043 square kilometers). This makes South Africa about two times the size of Texas. South Africa is divided into nine *provinces*. Each province is like a state in the United States. A province has its own government and leader. Marion Island and Prince Edward Island are also part of South Africa.

*Natal National Park*

South Africa's landscape is as beautiful as it is big. Three major landforms make up the country. In the center, there is a *plateau*. A plateau is high, flat land. Most of the South African plateau is between 4,000 and 6,000 feet (1,220 to 1,830 meters) high. On top of the plateau, there are rolling plains or grasslands called *highveld*. Most of South Africa's people and animals live on the highveld. Corn, wheat, fruits, and vegetables grow in its rich soil. Down deep below the soil, miners dig for gold, diamonds, and other precious minerals.

Mountain ranges surround the plateau on the east, south, and west. These mountain ranges are called the Great Escarpment. The peaks of the Drakenberg Mountains reach between 10,000 and 11,000 feet (3,050 to 3,350 m) high. They

*South African wildebeest*

seem to touch the clouds! Lush forests and *bushveld* cover the mountains. Krueger National Park's large animal reserve stretches across the land. A reserve is an area where animals are protected. Mammals known as Africa's Big Five—the elephant, lion, rhino, leopard, and buffalo—live safely on the reserve.

South Africa is located south of the *equator*. The seasons are opposite those in North America. When it is winter in the United States, it is summer in South Africa. The weather is the same throughout much of the country. Most days are mild, sunny, and dry. But along the coasts, ocean currents create differences in temperature and rainfall. The east coast is often warmer and wetter than the west coast.

In South Africa, scientists have discovered fossils that are 2.5 million years old. They have also dug up bones in the Sterkfontein Caves. The bones are believed to be from the earliest-known human. They are more than 100,000 years old. Because of these discoveries, South Africa is sometimes called the *Cradle of Civilization*.

# Table Mountain

There are no forks, spoons, or knives on this table! Table Mountain is a flattopped, sandstone mountain that overlooks Cape Town, South Africa. It is 3,000 feet (1,000 m) tall. Many South African residents and visitors hike, climb, or take cable cars to the top of the mountain. But exploring the mountain can be dangerous. Climbers must be careful. Weather conditions can change quickly on the mountain. Fast-moving rainstorms have soaked table-toppers. Others have been covered by Table Mountain's "tablecloth." This thin layer of clouds and fog often hangs over the mountain. But, whatever the weather, it is well worth the trip. After all, it is the only table you can stand on to enjoy breathtaking views of Cape Town, South Africa's oldest city.

# What Makes South Africa South African?

**S**outh Africa is like a giant jigsaw puzzle. It has millions of different pieces. These pieces come in many different shapes, sizes, colors, ethnic backgrounds, languages, and religions. Some pieces fit together. Others do not. South Africa's wide cultural differences make its people unique and special. These differences have also kept them apart.

*Schoolboys in Johannesburg*

*South Africans come from many different backgrounds.*

For many years, black, colored (or mixed race), and Asian people were not treated the same as white people. White South Africans ruled all of South Africa. From 1948 until the early 1990s, the South African government followed laws that separated whites from all the others. This was called *apartheid*, which means separateness. Under apartheid, nonwhites had to carry special passes to go into white areas. They were moved from their homes and forced to live in poor *townships*. Blacks were not allowed to be real citizens. They could not vote in elections. Black, colored, and Asian children had poor schools. By law, whites were given the best

*A young girl stands in the doorway of her home.*

jobs. Public rest rooms, restaurants, and other services were labeled "White only." That meant nonwhites were not allowed to use them.

Over the years, there were fights against apartheid. Young and old people protested. Many were killed or sent to jail. A black South African leader named Nelson Mandela worked hard to stop apartheid. He was arrested and sent to jail for twenty-seven years. In 1990, Mandela was freed. He continued to fight for equal rights for all South Africans. Soon after, apartheid came to an end. Nonwhite South Africans won the right to vote. They elected Mandela as the first black president of South Africa. Mandela made many changes. He provided more money for education, health care, and housing for the poorest South Africans. Today, South Africa is a *democratic republic*. But even though apartheid is against the law, racism still continues.

South Africa has been called the Rainbow Nation because it is a country of many colors. Seventy-five percent of South Africans are blacks. The largest number of black South Africans includes the Xhosa, Zulu, and Sotho people. White South Africans make up 13 percent of South Africans. They came more than 100 years ago from the Netherlands, Britain, France, and Germany.

Coloreds and Asians make up the rest of the South African population. Nine percent of South Africans are

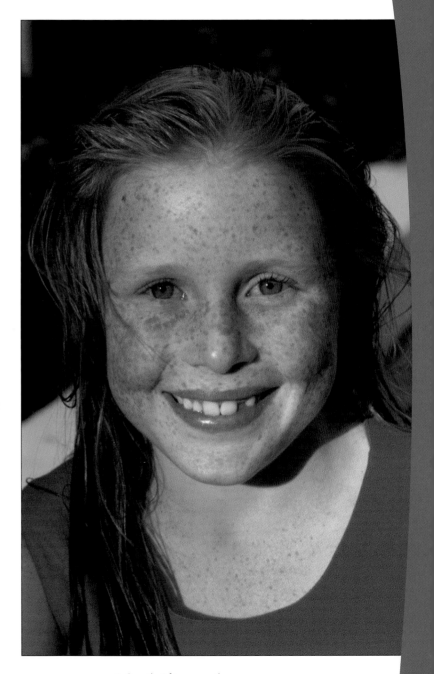

*A South African smile*

*A Christian church*

coloreds. They are the descendants of white settlers, Africans, and Asians. Three percent of South Africans are Asian. They came mostly from India.

As many as 68 percent of South Africans are Christian. They are Protestants and Catholics. Twenty-nine percent of South Africans follow African religions. Some South Africans hold both Christian and traditional African religious beliefs. A few South Africans are Muslims, Hindus, and Jews.

The most popular languages in South Africa are Zulu, Afrikaans, and English. Afrikaans came from the first Dutch settlers. Many South Africans speak at least two languages—their native language and English. English is spoken mostly at work and in school. Most South African street signs are in English.

South Africans are creative. They are writers, poets, musicians, actors, dancers, and artists. South African authors have written many novels, poems, and short stories about their country. Their works describe South Africa's beauty, history, culture, myths, and legends.

*South African singers*

South African musicians play blues, jazz, folk, hip-hop, and reggae. Actors perform on stage or on film in dramas, musicals, and classical operas. Dancers mix many styles of dance, including traditional, multicultural, and ballet. Artists re-create the beauty of South Africa's landscape or the pain of apartheid. Their work is displayed in galleries throughout the country. Some artists live in rural villages. They make quilts, baskets, clothing, beaded jewelry, dolls, and leather crafts.

*A doll made in a rural village*

# Rock Art

The first South Africans, called the San, were great artists. They engraved, or carved, and painted pictures on large rocks in caves or on mountains. Their pictures tell stories of hunters, animals, important events, warriors, and South Africa's first people. This rock art is among the earliest known in Africa. Some of it is 28,000 years old! Engravings that are more than 10,000 years old have been found in South Africa. The oldest painted stones are 6,400 years old. You could say that the caves and mountains of Africa were the world's first art galleries.

# Living in South Africa

Life in South Africa is full of contrasts. South Africans are rich or poor. They live in the city or the country. Some live in big, modern homes. Others live in small homes or shacks. For the most part, where people live depends on their race.

*Houses along a brick road*

During apartheid, whites ruled South Africa. They lived in beautiful homes with telephones, electricity, and running water. Some homes even had swimming pools. Their communities had the best schools, hospitals, and police departments. They also had shopping centers, playgrounds, and theaters.

Today, whites still have the nicest homes and jobs. They live and work throughout South Africa. They have jobs in education, business, mining, and police and fire departments.

*At home in a Johannesburg settlement*

*Fishermen pull in their nets.*

During apartheid, black, colored, and Asian South Africans were forced to live in very poor townships. They usually lived in homes without electricity or running water. They had poor schools. It was hard for them to get jobs. Many did not have enough money to buy food or to go to the doctor. After apartheid, some people left the townships to start a better life. Today, they are farmers, fishermen, miners,

*A miner drills in a deep mine.*

and construction workers. A few are accountants, lawyers, and teachers. Others continue to live in African townships and in poor rural areas. Many homes still do not have electricity or running water. Their communities have poor schools and services.

Some blacks often work on white farms raising cattle, sheep, and crops. Many must leave home to work in the cities. Women must care for their homes and families all alone. Since apartheid ended, the new South African government has worked to improve conditions for the poorest people. They want to provide them with better schools, homes, and jobs.

*Zulu women in traditional dress*

Many South Africans dress like people in North America. Others wear traditional clothing for holidays, festivals, and dances. They can choose from a variety of styles. With so many different backgrounds, South Africans may also choose meals from around the world. These meals may include English, French, German, Dutch, and Indian foods.

*South African boys dressed in jeans and T-shirts*

For breakfast, most South Africans enjoy *porridge* with coffee or tea and a *beskuit* (biscuit). Sandwiches and *bredies* (beef stews) make a good lunch. Hollow loaves of bread filled with bredies are lunchtime favorites.

Dinners include meats like lamb, beef, goat, or fish. South Africans especially love their meat cooked at barbecues or *brais*. *Boboties* (lamb casseroles), *sosaties*

*Biltong is a popular snack.*

(meat on skewers), and *samosas* (potato turnovers with curry) are favorites. Many South Africans also eat cornmeal or *sorghum* porridge with milk and vegetables, such as spinach or carrots. Tomatoes, cabbages, and other vegetables are popular side dishes. *Biltong*, a dried, spiced meat, is a favorite snack. When South Africans are thirsty, they drink milk, coffee, tea, or soda. After dinner, families may enjoy the outdoors.

# Let's Eat!
## Putu-pap (Cornmeal porridge)

Cornmeal porridge is a popular South African meal. Ask an adult to help you prepare this recipe.

**Ingredients:**

3 cups boiling water

2 teaspoons salt

1 pound fine white cornmeal

$1/2$ cup cold water

Wash your hands. Boil three cups of water in a medium-sized pot. Pour the cornmeal in a pile into the water and add salt. Do not stir. Remove the pot from the stove. Cover and let sit for five minutes. Uncover and stir. Then return the pot to the stove and simmer over low heat until the ingredients are crumbly. Stir again, adding cold water. Simmer for thirty minutes more. Serve with vegetables or gravy.

# School Days

Education is important in South Africa. South Africans believe that school will help young people have better lives and brighter futures. All children must attend school from ages seven to fifteen. Parents encourage their children to study and do well in school.

Over the years, education in South Africa has changed. During apartheid, most of the money for schools went to white schools. The separate schools for black, colored, and Asian children did not receive much money. They had untrained teachers, few supplies, and too many children in each classroom.

Today, some of the schools are integrated, or mixed. The government is working hard to build better schools for all children. It has also created a National Curriculum to teach all of its children the same subjects. Better schools will help more children attend college and get jobs. But there is still a

*Students at an integrated school*

lot to do to make schools throughout South Africa equal.

In South Africa, there are three levels of school: primary, secondary, and university. Primary schools have two cycles that each last three years. First through third grades are called the junior cycle. In these grades, students learn reading, writing, math, and two languages—their own and another. The senior cycle is fourth through sixth grade. Senior cycle students study reading, math, languages, geography, and science.

Secondary school, or high school, is for grades seven through twelve. Some students attend all six years. Others may attend only until ninth grade. Many of these students must leave school to help

*Classmates*

*In a secondary school classroom*

*Students perform science experiments.*

support their families. Some choose to leave school to learn job skills or take computer classes. Others finish secondary school in hopes of going on to college or a technical school.

In high school, students must pass a special test to graduate and earn the senior certificate. Students' test scores will help decide whether or not they will continue their education. Some will attend a university, college, or technical school. After college, graduates may choose to work in a variety of jobs. Some may choose to teach South Africa's future students and help make their schools even better.

# South Africanisms

In cities across South Africa, people use many common sayings every day. They are called *South Africanisms*. These sayings are a blend of South Africans' colorful languages. Amaze your friends and family. Work some of them into your conversations—*now now now*!

| | |
|---|---|
| *Baie dankie* | Thank you very much. |
| *Bonsella* | A gift or a tip |
| *Howzit* | How are you? |
| *Izzit* | Oh, really? |
| *Ja-nee* | Maybe |
| *Jong* | Young fellow |
| *Just now* | Recently, in a while |
| *Lekker* | Nice, enjoyable |
| *Mampara* | A fool |
| *Now now* | In a little while |
| *Now now now* | Immediately, instantly |
| *Tula* | Be quiet |
| *Totsiens* | Good-bye |
| *Vasbyt* | Hang in there |
| *Voetsek, voetsak* | Go away |
| *Wag 'n bietjie* | Wait a minute |
| *Winkel* | A shop |

# Just for Fun

South Africans love to play and watch sports. They follow their favorite teams very closely. They cheer them on in victory and in defeat. Wherever there is open land and a ball, there is a game going on.

South Africa's favorite sports are rugby, cricket, and soccer. Rugby is like soccer, except players can use their hands. Cricket is similar to baseball, but players use wickets instead of bats. In the past, only white South Africans played rugby and cricket. Today South Africans of all colors are beginning to play and watch these sports. Soccer is a sport played by all in South Africa. That is why it

*South African rugby players make a tackle!*

*Cricket players in action*

is called "the people's game." Other favorite sports in South Africa include track and field, basketball, and field hockey.

During apartheid, only whites were allowed to play professional sports. The rest of the world thought this was unfair. Because of this, South Africa was not allowed to play international sports. Since the end of apartheid, South African sports teams have been invited to compete in world events again. The rugby

*A soccer match in South Africa*

team, the Springboks, won the rugby World Cup in 1995. The cricket team won the African Cup of Nations in 1996. The soccer team called Bafana Bafana (The boys, the boys) won the African Cup of Nations in 1996. The team also reached the finals of the World Cup in 1998. South Africans are also world-class surfers, golfers, boxers, swimmers, and tennis players. At the Olympics, athletes have won medals in swimming and marathons.

When South Africans are not playing or watching sports, they enjoy the great outdoors. The country's pleasant weather and landscapes offer many choices for outdoor fun.

*A breathtaking view of South Africa's landscape*

Hiking, cycling, mountaineering, exploring, and sight-seeing are all favorite activi-
ties. Boaters, rafters, swimmers, surfers, fishermen, divers, water-skiers, and
sunbathers splash through the oceans, rivers, and streams. People explore the
many national parks, gardens, and animal reserves to see South Africa's unique

*Bikers at Lone Creek Falls*

plants and animals. Golfers can take a swing at South Africa's many golf courses. Horseback riding, running, shopping, and dancing at discos and nightclubs are also favorite South African pastimes.

Whatever South Africans do for fun, their love of sports brings them together. No matter what color or religion, they play and cheer side by side. Sports have helped ease racial problems in South Africa. Many hope that sports will also help to unite South Africa.

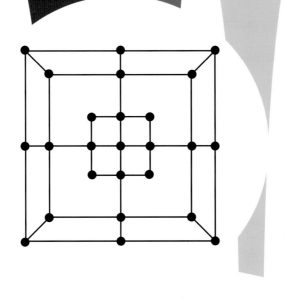

# Morabaraba

Morabaraba is the oldest—and one of the most popular—board games in South Africa. Forty percent of the country plays Morabaraba. It is even recognized as a South African sport! To play Morabaraba, you need two players, twenty-four game pieces, one game board, and two brains. This game requires a lot of thinking.

Each player receives twelve game pieces called cows. They take turns placing their cows, one at a time, on the points on the game board (shown above). The object of the game is to make a row of three cows, as in tic-tac-toe. This is called a strike. When a player makes a strike, he can remove one of his opponent's cows. When a player cannot move his cows or he has only two cows left, the other player wins.

Legend has it that African chiefs taught their young warriors the game to assure successful cattle raids. Other stories say that chiefs asked Morabaraba winners for advice. Today, teachers encourage students to play Morabaraba. They believe it helps students focus, think, and celebrate their African heritage.

# Let's Celebrate!

South Africans know how to celebrate. Each year is filled with many religious and national holidays, and with festivals. Whether it is in a village or a city, South Africans spend holidays with family and friends. Many attend church services and eat big meals.

Since most South Africans are Christian, Christmas and Easter are two of the most important religious holidays. At Christmas, they celebrate the birth of Jesus. Families travel long distances to spend the holiday together. They go to church, exchange gifts, and eat together. Boys and girls may sing Christmas carols or perform in plays.

On Easter Sunday, Christians attend church services, pray, and sing. Like Christmas, the day is spent with family and friends.

Muslims observe Ramadan. It is a holiday filled with prayer and fasting. Adult Muslims do not eat or drink from sunrise to sunset for thirty

*This Christmas tree stands near a mosque where Muslims pray.*

*A New Year's carnival*

*Happy New Year!*

days. When Ramadan is over, Muslims celebrate Id-al-fitr. It is the end of the fast. Id-al-fitr is celebrated with music, dance, food, and gifts.

National holidays also fill South Africa's calendars. New Year's Day is celebrated with a historic neighborhood parade. On Youth Day, South Africans remember the black students who began a major movement to end apartheid. National Woman's Day honors the 20,000 women who marched to Pretoria to demand equal rights for all South Africans.

Some South African holidays, such as Freedom Day, are new since the end of apartheid. Freedom Day marks the day that blacks and coloreds won the right to vote. The Day of Reconciliation is a day to forgive the past hurts of apartheid. Heritage Day celebrates the new South Africa.

*Children celebrate the National Day of Peace.*

On national holidays, government offices and many businesses are closed. South Africans enjoy spending time with family and friends. Some may play sports, go shopping, or visit the country's parks, animal reserves, or museums.

Throughout the year, there are music and arts festivals. Three major South African festivals include the Grahamstown Festival, the Splashy Fen, and the Rustler's Valley. Every July, the Grahamstown Festival has theater, art, music, and comedy shows. In spring, the Splashy Fen presents rock, folk, and other popular music on a farm in Underberg. The Rustler's Valley is held on top of the Wittenberg Mountains. Here, the cool sounds of African jazz and traditional music blend with the warm African weather.

# Youth Day, June 16

South Africa celebrates Youth Day on June 16. This day honors the young black South African students who died protesting apartheid. Their protests helped end apartheid. They also paved the way for a new South African government. The first protests began in Soweto, South Africa, on June 16, 1976. In the months that followed, almost 1,000 protesters were killed.

For many years before the end of apartheid, Youth Day was a day of sorrow and grief. People mourned the loss of young lives. Today, the holiday still honors those who died. But it is also a day filled with hope for the future. Wreaths honor the young people who fought against apartheid. Speeches and other festivities are planned.

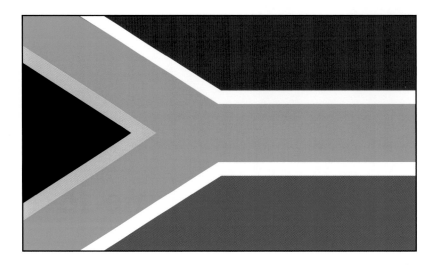

South Africa's flag has six colors: green, black, white, gold, red, and blue. These colors come from past flags of both black and white South Africans. The flag includes two bands that meet in the middle to make one. This design stands for the new unity in South Africa. It also follows the South African motto: "Unity is strength." The flag was adopted in April 1994.

South Africa's money is called the rand. In July 2003, one rand was equal to thirteen U.S. cents.

# Count in Zulu

| English | Zulu | Say it like this: |
|---------|------|-------------------|
| one | kunye | KOO-yay |
| two | kubili | koo-BEE-lee |
| three | kuthathu | koo-TAH-too |
| four | kune | KOO-nay |
| five | isihlanu | is-ee-SHAH-noo |
| six | isithupha | is-TOO-pah |
| seven | isikhombisa | is-KOHM-bee-sah |
| eight | isishiyagalombili | IS-shee-en-on-oom-bee-lee |
| nine | isishiyagalolunye | is-SHEE-ada-loo-loon-yay |
| ten | ishumi | FSHOO-mee |

# Glossary

**apartheid** (uh-PAR-tide)   South African law that separated whites and nonwhites.

**bushveld**   Area of South Africa covered by shrubs and thorny plants.

**curriculum**   A program of study in school; the lessons taught to students.

**democratic republic**   A government in which the people elect their leaders.

**equator** (i-KWAY-tuhr)   The imaginary line around the middle of the Earth.

**highveld**   Rolling plains and grasslands.

**plateau** (pla-TOE)   An area of high, flat ground.

**porridge**   A breakfast cereal often made by boiling cornmeal or other grains in milk.

**province**   A district or region of South Africa.

**sorghum**   A sweet tropical grass or grain often used to make syrup and sugar.

# Fast Facts

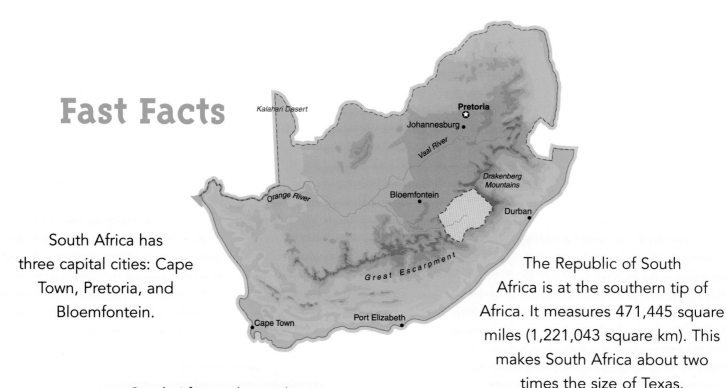

South Africa has three capital cities: Cape Town, Pretoria, and Bloemfontein.

The Republic of South Africa is at the southern tip of Africa. It measures 471,445 square miles (1,221,043 square km). This makes South Africa about two times the size of Texas.

South Africa is located south of the equator. The seasons are opposite those in North America. When it is winter in the United States, it is summer in South Africa.

Table Mountain is a flattopped, sandstone mountain overlooking Cape Town, South Africa. It is 3,000 feet (1,000 m) tall.

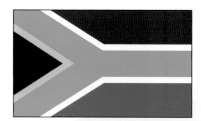

South Africa's flag has six colors: green, black, white, gold, red, and blue. These colors come from past flags of both black and white South Africans. Its design shows the new unity in South Africa.

Sixty-eight percent of South Africans are Christian, 2 percent are Muslim, 1.5 percent are Hindu, and 28.5 percent follow traditional African religions.

South Africa's money is called the rand. In July 2003, one rand was equal to thirteen U.S. cents.

As of July 2002, 43,647,658 people lived in South Africa.

From 1948 until the early 1990s, the South African government followed laws that separated white South Africans from nonwhite South Africans. This was called apartheid, or separateness.

South Africa's favorite sports are rugby, cricket, and soccer. Soccer is called the people's game.

In 1994, South Africa held its first free election. People of all races were allowed to vote. Today South Africa is a democratic republic. Apartheid is against the law.

The most popular languages in South Africa are Zulu, Afrikaans, and English.

# Proud to Be South African

## Dr. Christiaan N. Barnard (1922–2001)

Dr. Christiaan N. Barnard was born in 1922 in Beaufort West, Cape Province, South Africa. He was a world-famous heart surgeon. In 1967, Dr. Barnard was the first surgeon to transplant a human heart into another human being. He also discovered new ways to perform open-heart surgery. Dr. Barnard worked as a surgeon in Cape Town. He studied at the University of Minnesota in the United States. After medical school, he returned to South Africa to set up a heart unit in Cape Town. Because of Dr. Barnard's great skills, people with serious heart problems can live longer lives.

## Nadine Gordimer (1923–    )

Nadine Gordimer was born in 1923 in Springs, South Africa. She is a well-known novelist and short-story author. Gordimer's stories describe the people and places of South Africa. Gordimer began writing when she was young. Her teachers encouraged her to write. She published her first story at fifteen. Ten years later, she published a collection of short stories called *Face to Face*. Her first novel, *The Lying Days*, was published in 1953. Today, she has written twelve novels, nine books, and four collections of essays. Her work has won many honors and awards. During apartheid, three of her books were banned in South Africa. These books described the terrible conditions created by the government. Gordimer won the Nobel Prize for Literature in 1991. She was the first woman to win this award in twenty-five years.

## Nelson R. Mandela (1918–   )

Nelson R. Mandela was born in July of 1918 in Transkei, South Africa. He was the greatest force in the movement against apartheid. Mandela studied law and opened the first

black law firm in South Africa. In 1952, he headed the African National Congress. As a member, he used boycotts and strikes to fight for freedom for blacks. When nonviolent efforts did not work, his group used military force. He and other members of Congress were sent to jail. Mandela spent twenty-seven years in prison. He was freed in 1990. In 1994, the people elected Mandela to be the first black president of the Republic of South Africa. He began a democratic government and worked to create equality for all people. Nelson Mandela won the Nobel Peace Prize in 1993 for his fight against apartheid.

# Find Out More

## Books

*South Africa* by Alison Brownlie. Raintree Steck-Vaughn, Austin, TX, 2000.

*South Africa* by Laurel Corona. Lucent Books, San Diego, CA, 2000.

*South Africa* by Bruce Fish and Becky Durost Fish. Chelsea House Publishers, Philadelphia, PA, 2000.

*A Ticket to South Africa* by Mary N. Oluonye. Carolrhoda Books, Minneapolis, MN, 1999.

*Welcome to South Africa* by Meredith Costain and Paul Collins. Chelsea House Publishers, Philadelphia, PA, 2001.

## Web Sites

Embassy of South Africa
**www.saembassy.org**

South Africa: CIA Fact Book
**www.odci.gov/cia/publications/factbook/geos/sf.html**

## Video

*Going Places: South Africa*, Mpi Home Video, 1998.

# Index

Page numbers for illustrations are in **boldface.**

## About the Author

Patricia J. Murphy writes children's storybooks, nonfiction books, early readers, and poetry. She also writes for magazines, corporations, educational publishing companies, and museums. Patricia lives in Northbrook, Illinois. She hopes someday to go on a safari in South Africa.

## Acknowledgments

Special thanks to Jabu Mbewe of the South African Consulate in Chicago, the South African Embassy, the South African Tourism Bureau, Susan Kovacs at the Arlington Heights Memorial Library, and Vaughn Smith.